From Heartache to Hope

CATHY EVANS

From Heartache to Hope
By Cathy Evans

ISBN: 9798797528333

TABLE OF CONTENTS

When I think of Cathy and the journey she has walked these past four years, Psalm 23 is what comes to my mind. Cathy's story of navigating through the grief and heartbreak in the loss of her husband to cancer, is one of great courage. I deeply admire Cathy's faith in her loving Heavenly Father, whom she calls Papa, and Jesus, the shepherd of her soul, who guided her on this journey of healing. Cathy has beautifully put into words with sheer transparency her heart's cry for the answers that only an all wise and knowing God can bring. Cathy learned to trust in His unfailing Love, holding onto His hand through the darkest valley of her life. I don't know many people who have come through the loss of a loved one quite like Cathy has. She didn't let grief master her, but through the tears and pain she rose up in renewed trust in a faithful and loving God.

Through her deep intimacy with Papa, Cathy has experienced healing and restoration in her broken soul, and great hope awaits in her future. You will be blessed by Cathy's powerful poetic writing and the spirit of wisdom that she imparts.

You can believe again! You can hope again! It's time to live again!!

Pastor Sue Sherstad
Co-author of The Miracle Effect

FOREWORD

Pastors Michael and Robin Shaver

We have been blessed to know & serve the Lord with Cathy for about 15 years. We have watched her mature into the woman of God that she is today.

This book may stir up many emotions surrounding the difficult journey that we walked through with Cathy and her husband (Keith), but it also shows the perseverance of a heart totally sold out to Papa God. During the time of Keith's battle with cancer, Cathy may have had her struggles (as anyone would) but she never gave up on God's Truth.

As her spiritual parents, the best thing we could do for her was be there to listen, to pray with her and love on her. She could only receive true healing from the Lord himself.

Keith was faithful to the Lord and never lost focus despite what he was going through physically. Reading these glimpses of what Cathy was going through and what God was teaching her through it all is inspiring. She has the victory in spite of what the enemy tried to do to her.

We are blessed to have Cathy in our lives & in our ministry. We are very grateful that she has overcome so she can share this journey with others. This book does an excellent job of showing how God will bring healing even in the midst of some of the worst of life's circumstances.

Blessings,
Pastors Michael & Robin Shaver
Servant's Heart Fellowship
Peru, Illinois

1

Where Fear Meets Faith

One of the fears of life that tormented me was losing you. I couldn't imagine life without you. I believed that we would grow old together, do ministry together and face life together. I remember that day when life stood still as the doctor was telling us what was going on. It felt as if all the voices and weeping became silent, as fear tried to grip my soul. I couldn't put words together. Only these words came up out of my spirit: "He will live and not die and declare the works of the Lord." I said that over and over as I walked through the hospital halls, as it built strength in me. I wouldn't allow any doctor to come in and speak anything else, nor would I listen to anything else. I fought against every negative word spoken with the word of God, knowing He alone carried all power to turn this all around. One thing remained true: He wouldn't go against the will of one of

His children. I remember the atmosphere had changed in you, around you and around healing. It was right after one of the biggest surgeries you endured. You really hadn't spoken much about anything until one night in our bedroom you began to share what happened. While having that surgery Jesus came to you and took you to heaven. He walked with you, just talking, and showing you the amazing places He longed for you to see. Then He took you into the throne room, and there you heard worship like you had never heard before. It drove you to your knees. You said it was the most beautiful sound that your ears ever heard and nothing on earth could compare to it. You then went on to say Jesus asked you stay. You wanted to stay, but you had some things that needed to be taken care of down here. He smiled at you, then you woke up in your room. The peace I saw on you then was like nothing I had ever seen. Even though you fought to live, nothing could compare to the life you felt in His presence. I believe during those 6 months your heart was changed, and faith was stronger than ever. His presence humbled both of us through that journey. I think you knew all along that He wanted you to come back to Him, and your journey on this earth was almost finished. You encouraged all our faith and trusted Papa to the very end of your journey here on this earth. Your whole perspective changed and things that were so important before became so dim in His presence.

I look back almost 4 years ago and now sit at a place of totally different perspective. I have walked through so many questions, anger, and deep sadness. I thought at one point my life was over, and honestly, it was over. That part of life's journey had ended, and Papa had something new.

I'm so grateful for our life together, but I'm also grateful for this new beginning. It is a new beginning of a new journey to see His kingdom come upon the earth as it is in heaven.

I felt my heart break in a million pieces, only to feel His touch putting it back together. In that moment my heart stopped, only for me to tell it to beat again to the rhythm of His.

A lot of things have changed, but through it all His grace has abounded to me. His love saturates every piece of me, allowing me to grow beyond anything I could ever imagine. I am becoming who He created me to be, knowing He will never let me go. Sadness has been replaced with joy, heartache with peace and death with life. What a great God I serve!

What was once lost has been found and identity is being revealed. Strength has come to embrace me and envelop every part of me. I'm not the woman I thought I was. I am the little girl who still runs into her Papa God's arms as He whispers my worth in my ear. I miss you.

The Spring of 2016 started out with some home projects: Painting the house and refreshing the landscape. The kids all helped, even the grandkids. It was such a fun start to the warmer months. I remember how tired you were, not feeling well, and just chalked it up to working a lot. Little did we know that by the end of the year our whole world would crash down around us and God's love and who He is would become our strength and our song.

I look back at that time and see how Papa prepared us for what were going to be life changing events. As spring turned to summer, we noticed even more how tired and how nauseous you were, and how blisters started forming on your body and in your mouth.

As summer turned to fall, your symptoms got worse. You started throwing up randomly and out of nowhere, but Babe, that never stopped you from going to work! We took many trips to the ER to get an IV to replenish all you had lost from throwing up. They did blood tests and said there was something going on but didn't quite know what it was. They never did a CAT scan or anything else until much later. You would get rehydrated and off you went to work, without a care in the world. Your faith shined through on the darkest days. I remember the day you asked me to take pictures of your blisters. You said "Babe, I want proof of the healing that God did when all of these disappear. Nothing shook you. You knew who you were and to Whom you belonged.

As fall approached so did many of the symptoms that had you sidelined. As October turned into November there were more times at the ER. When Thanksgiving came and you couldn't even eat, we were both concerned. It started to become even more real to us that something deeper was going on. You never let that stop you from going to your grandkids' events. At Gwen's parade at the Festival of Lights, you were weak from not really eating, but you had to be there. By that point, you had lost 40 pounds and eating was not even a desire. Your work began to suffer, as you had to stop every 15 to 20 minutes to vomit and lay flat. The pain was becoming more difficult for you to hide.

2

A Journey's Hope

We tried to get you in to see many doctors to find out what was going on. We finally got in to see Dr. D., and she ordered some tests. They found water in your belly and a little more. She wanted to talk to us, but we never made it to the next appointment. On Dec 9th I took you to the ER. The night before, you were in so much pain, tossing and turning. You came out to sleep on the couch to spare me from waking up, but I followed you in there and prayed for you. You finally drifted off to sleep before having to wake up and go to work. I told you when you got home, we were going to the ER to find out what was going on. You agreed to go. As soon as your boots hit the porch, I was warming the car to take you. You laughed and said, "All right, all right, let's go." As we drove, you shared with me that you looked up why you would have water on your belly.

I told you I did the same. Then we were silent the rest of the way to the hospital. Neither of us even wanted to go there in our conversation.

It was a Friday night we would have been going to church. A night full of excitement as we gathered to worship, but we were at the hospital waiting to hear what they were going to do. They found out your appendix was leaking, and the doctor was going to do laparoscopic surgery to find out what damage had been done from it leaking. I remember that all of us gathered in your room as our pastors came and prayed over you. The room filled up with His presence, which brought His peace. It was so late when they took you into surgery. I remember walking the halls that night, asking Papa to hold you and us as we waited for the doctor. When the doctor came out, he told us your whole belly was filled with cancer. He showed us the pictures, and he didn't give us much hope. He was so blunt, without any compassion. We were all numb, hearing that news. He said it was stage 4 cancer and a big tumor was blocking your stomach. There was no way any food could even get into your intestines, and something would have to be done right away.

They took me back to the ICU where you lay recovering. You looked up at me and said, "I'm good Babe," but little did you know what was going on. I didn't know how I was going to tell you. I think we were all in such disbelief, weeping and crying, just holding on to one another. All the life was sucked out of the room. It was about 1:00 a.m. when we headed back to your room, and everyone started to leave. I remember getting on the elevator and telling Satan, "You're not taking my husband. He will live and not die!" As I walked the hospital halls, I wouldn't let go of

His truth, nor would I allow anyone to speak negative words around you, not even the doctors.

I believe there comes a point in this life's journey where you stop in the middle of the road and wonder, "How did I get here?" How did I get through all of that? You stop to take a breath and take it all in, because only God knows how He will get you through.

I can recall days and nights where the ground beneath my feet gave way, and I felt as if I was spiraling down, making it just to the top of the water, not being able to keep treading and losing all the air around me as I tried to breathe, feeling crushed by hopelessness, sadness, and fear. Every step I took I knew He was with me. He never left my side and even when I couldn't call out to Him, He made known His presence to me in the simplest of ways. His love would come rushing in and overwhelm me with His peace, the peace that wraps you up in love and drives out all that tries to stand against it.

There were times when I felt like I couldn't do another thing, I couldn't fake it anymore, and my strength failed. It was in those times that His strength was truly made known to me. He carried me when I couldn't even crawl. His was that voice that encouraged me that He was making a way and His was the touch that held me together.

There were days I would weep and weep, and He held me close. Have you ever felt Him hold you? Ask Holy Spirit to come as you close your eyes and take a deep breath in, as you rest in the silence, and you hear Him whisper. *Write down on the lines below what you hear Him speaking to your heart…*

3
His Strength

I think back on how the Lord kept us in the days that lay ahead of us. I remember how He prepared our every step. He never left us, not even for a moment. When we got to the ER on Dec 9, 2016, we never thought it would be a journey that left us in hospitals for months.

I remember you waking up and you asked what was going on. I tried to tell you, but you were in and out of it. The next morning, we talked, and then the flood of doctors came in with fears and concerns. By that evening we were all alone, and I started to play worship music. We both broke, weeping and being held by Papa. His presence permeated that room and every part of us.

That night the nurse came in and made sure you were comfortable. She redid your IV bags, she turned off your overhead light and walked over to me and asked if I needed anything. I never looked up. I just started weeping, and she came over to the side of the bed and held me. No words were spoken. She just sat there and held me until everything that was in me came out in my tears. I knew Jesus was in that room comforting us. He used that nurse to help me release what was in my heart. The doctors came in, day in and day out, trying to figure out how to get the huge tumor removed from your stomach and small intestines.

They decided to have you go to St Frances. The night we left, you went in the ambulance, and I drove. It was an icy mess, and I had no idea where I was going. I remember I was crying so hard and approached some girls that worked at the hospital. I drove up and said, "Please help me. I need to get to my husband." I know Papa had them there just for me. One of the girls calmed me and helped me get my car in the parking garage, and then took me to where you were. I waited for you and couldn't have been happier when they brought you in. That was going to be our home for the next few weeks.

We didn't know then, but we spent our last Christmas there, all together in that hospital room. The kids chipped in and got you the new Play Station 4. You were so surprised, and with tears in your eyes said, "You kids didn't have to do this." Oh Babe, they were so happy they could do that for you. It meant everything to them.

4
When the Journey Took Us Through the Deepest Valley

I remember those first days, finding out this journey we were both on with so many others that remained close by our sides. Papa made it so evident that we were not alone. His peace, strength and hope surrounded us like a thick wall of love. I remember praying in the halls, declaring His word over you and all the situations we were going to have to face. Throughout this journey we all learned more of who He is as He proved to be the arms we ran to when the overwhelming words from doctors came, the tower of
strength when our hearts became weak in sadness, and the strength when everything in us was so uncertain. I

remember every detail of His presence as He flooded us no matter where we were. You, my love, never lost sight of the journey ahead. You walked it with such strength and determination. Peace flowed from you even when sickness was surrounding you. Every beautiful moment that Papa gave us was so treasured.

Do you remember when you knew He was with you through a difficult time? Write it on the lines below.

As they did the surgery to remove some of the tumor and redirect your intestines to your stomach so that you could eat and get nourishment, something happened with you during that process. It was later that you told us that during the surgery Jesus came to you and took you to heaven. He took you into the throne room where the worship was like nothing you ever heard on this earth. Its sounds permeated every part of you. Jesus then looked at you and asked you to stay. You wanted to but said to Him, "There are some things I need to take care of on the earth." So, He allowed you to come back, but as I look back on that, I can see how much you loved being there with Him. There was such a peace with you and a humbling in your soul that had changed you.

Through the next several weeks you began to heal from the surgery. You were able to come home for two days and then we ended up back in the ER because your incision was leaking. That's when things started to get real. There were many more visits to the hospital and having to stay there, then there was home. We grew homesick many days, missing our kids, our grandkids, and our church family. It was definitely a time of maturing in our spirits as we trusted God to bring the results that we believed He would. Many nights I would sit in the chair by your bed as I sought God for answers.

I always went to Papa with barrels blazing, reminding Him of all the promises and the healing scriptures that He wrote. I had a strategy to come against the enemy and continue to speak life into your being. God was so gracious to me in those days as I told Him what needed to be done with you. Then one day as I began to decree His Word, this was the conversation that stopped me in my tracks:

I ran into Your presence with the battle plan ready to engage the enemy and take back the land. My mind was racing as my words were filled with Your truth, looking all around, but I couldn't find You. The silence gripped my heart as I heard Your whisper, "Child can we just play today? Would you run into My arms as I bounce you on My knee? Can we shut out the world and all its screaming? I want to run through the fields as the dew moistens our fingertips and sets off a fragrance that can only come when your heart is free like a fragrant perfume. Your laughter sets the pace as your heart begins to overflow with all the child-like dreams that I kept safe. Do you remember? I listened to all you had to say when excitement was fresh. It took your breath away. Can We stay in this moment where you are free to dream as you search My heart and believe again?"

The sounds of heaven, electrified by the garments of praise that flow from your lips from all the love have been released from the inside. Nothing pulls or takes your gaze away. Just this moment in your presence is why My heart breaks. Oh, that your laughter would fill the atmosphere with the giggles that have been hidden under the weight of the world's despair. Can you just let it all go to be with Me, allowing My love to give your heart wings, allowing My breath to bring new life to all the broken dreams as you fly higher than you ever dreamed? Can you focus on the promises we once shared, when coming into My presence was fun and filled with excitement without a care?

Can you just come and lay at My feet, so I can fill your heart with all I want you to see? The war that rages is all under My feet. It's time, My child, to just sit and breathe. Today I long for you to be hidden in My presence, allowing your heart to be free, running through My garden, filling your soul with every piece of Me."

Have you ever been in that place where everything surrounding you was taking your focus off Him? *In the lines below write down what captured your focus…*

___

___

___

___

___

___

___

___

___

___

___

___

___

My whole focus was on Keith's healing and battling the enemy, instead of focusing on Him. Ouch! He longed for me to just be with Him, to rest in His presence and be refreshed. He knew the days ahead would be filled with such turmoil, sleeplessness, and a testing of our faith like we had never seen before.

One thing I have really learned throughout this journey is that resting, sitting, and listening at His feet will give you the battle plan. Instead of wearing yourself out with what you think you should do when crisis comes, when your whole world is shattered, and hope is nowhere to be found, it's good to have a reservoir filled with His presence and peace. Let's talk a moment about how to fill your reservoir. spending time in His Word and in His presence daily will give you the strength, endurance, and faith to see through any situation that comes your way. You will learn to draw strength from Him and His promises more than relying on yourself and what you think will get you through. Trust me in this, He knows the beginning to the end when we only see what is in the moment.

My thoughts were, "If I decree enough, if I believe enough, if I pray enough, then Keith will be all right. He will live and not die and declare the works of the Lord." That was one of the verses I stood on every day and every night, in every situation. Even when doctors would come with their bad news, I wouldn't let them speak it over him. My mind was only one dimensional and what I thought I knew became a road and a journey to hear the voice of the Lord. I want to tell you that if you are struggling with understanding the plan that God has for you or what you are going through, sit, listen, and wait in His presence.

Write down what He speaks to you on the lines below. Practice listening and not just hearing…

5
Pause In His Presence

In the most devastating times, we often feel so alone and maybe even abandoned. We begin to rely on what we see and how we feel to get us through. We allow ourselves to grow numb, senseless to the pain we are feeling. Perhaps it's because we don't understand why bad things happen and lose sight of the One who holds all our tomorrows. It takes our breath and focus, and we begin to live in survival mode. Our focus becomes blurry and the talking in our head becomes louder than His voice. He tries to get us to see He is with us in all the little things along the way, but in that moment our eyes see only what is in front of us and not Who is inside us.

I remember so many times when I stopped and took a moment to breathe, that amid all the chaos He invited me to close my eyes, rest in His arms and breathe in His presence. All the noise on the journey will try to take you under and cause weariness to overtake you. It's in these moments when life is a blur, if we choose to take a moment (which could lead into a lot of moments) and call out His name, He comes running to us, picks us up and holds us close to His heart. Then we can see He is there to strengthen us along the way, to breathe peace into our lungs, and focus on His promises through the most crucial times in our lives. Pause for a moment, close your eyes. What is He saying to your heart? *On the lines below, write down what He is saying…*

6
When Running Leads You Into His Arms

The next few months were hopeful as we went to CCOA. We just knew this was a step Papa would use to do what He was going to do in you. They were the best of the best for this type of cancer. We would stay there for days, weeks and months as they did your treatments. We were rarely home from January to April. With many setbacks in your health and new situations popping up, there would be great challenges.

Those days were so taxing on both of us as we grew so weary in the waiting. There came a point where you were so weak you couldn't walk much and were so sick from all the treatments you couldn't eat, and at some point, you couldn't drink, which caused so many problems.

We were tired since we had been awake for days. Growing testy with each other, I found myself on many occasions in the elevator, saying the name of Jesus over and over. I couldn't quiet myself; I was struggling with so many emotions. It was overwhelming.

No matter where I found myself in those days, I ran to the only One who could hold my heart and myself together and calm the fears that tormented me. I saw you turning into someone I didn't recognize anymore. You grew quiet, but peace was so evident in your soul.

As I sat in the chair while you drifted off to sleep, I felt a depth of sadness that I had never felt before. I tried to fight it with the Word of God, but I grew weary. I laid my head back and wept quietly when these words overwhelmed my soul and peace saturated our room: Psalms 33:18, *"The LORD is near to the brokenhearted and saves those who are crushed in spirit."* He is so close you can feel His breath.

I never knew sadness could go so deep. Minutes turned to hours, hours to days, days to months, months to years. Time stood still. It stopped its hands in my heart. My soul had been quieted within me, seeking for the peace that only His love can bring. He waits in the room where my silence is deafening. He listens to my tears as they hit my pillow in the night, waiting for me to say His name. Yet I waited, thinking I could deal with this pain on my own. He sang over me His song of hope as I lay with the questions that overwhelmed my soul. I spoke as He held my head and collected my tears telling me they were not in vain. He knew my anger as I had tried to hide it and told me of our story He has written just for me. He invited me to rest as He washed over my soul and put His fingerprints on the places I needed to let go. The what-ifs, should-haves and could-have-beens seemed to melt away in His loving embrace. He is never harsh, although some of my words to Him are. He just holds me close and tells me to let it all out again. I asked Him why grieving was such a painful thing. He looked in my eyes and reached deep into my soul and told me the story of His love and how He wouldn't ever let me go. He said that grieving was never part of His plan, and that He runs to those whose hearts have been hurting and bare, knowing His love longs to take care. He told me He runs when He hears the heart-cries of someone that is broken and speaks life into their season. He brings the hope that has seemed to disappear and fills it in time with what He longs to share. As I lay down to sleep, He is so close to me even if I can't feel Him. I choose to believe.

I closed my eyes and drifted to sleep, awaiting the news the doctors would bring. It felt like we were constantly in transition, never knowing what would come next. I know Papa was holding both of our hands as I asked Him to help me see what it looked like from His perspective.

Have you ever felt like everything was running out of control and you couldn't stop it? To what or whom do you run? *On the lines below share your thoughts…*

____

____

____

Can I encourage you to run into the arms of the One who knows you best, the One who can handle your anger, frustration, and fears?

7
When Anger Rises, So Does His Grace

I walked into this place knowing I would not leave here the same. I knew in my heart the anger and all the silent screams were about to explode out of this heart that was broke. I spoke but never uttered a word. I came at you with fist's pounding on Your chest wanting the why's to be answered, the what if's to stop shouting in my mind knowing You were the only One who held the answers to all my unbelief. I shouted with pain and cried tears of frustration. How could this be real? Why didn't You do something? I believed, I trusted and spoke out Your truth. Why didn't Your word come to pass? Why didn't You do what You said You would do? Why didn't You save my heart from all it went through?

My words became loud and filled with such pain as my heart was emptied of all that was hidden deep. You held Me tight. No words did You speak as all the poison in my heart began to leak. You never got angry. You never spoke a word. You just opened Your arms and let me weep bitterly. You stood there as I beat upon Your chest letting You know my heart was not at rest.

That day I was real with You and with Myself, not holding anything back. I was so tired of the unrest. I fell to the ground with no strength left, wrestling with the ideas that were still in my head. When You knelt down, taking my head into Your hands, You spoke these words that echoed through my soul, "Trust in Me with all your heart and lean not to your own understanding; In all your ways acknowledge Me and I will direct your steps. I will never leave you nor forsake you. Child you are mine. My love for you will sustain you in this season. Being real will open you up to allow My healing waters to flow to every part!

He spoke; I listened and there we sat, picking up the broken pieces of a life that was spent. He hears, He sees, and He knows. At times we might feel He is far away, but it's in those times He is closer than your skin.

So many things throughout this six-month journey had prepared me to let go. Holy Spirit was leading us, all of us, to let go and trust God. We faced another surgery; this one was to help you get nourishment to make you stronger and more able to continue with the chemo. You couldn't eat or drink anything at this time. It just stuck like glue in your intestines, not going any farther, as it was supposed to do.

I remember that day you passed out when I was giving you a shower. I thought you had a seizure, but little did we know it was because your electrolytes were all out of whack, and nothing was giving you the nutrition you needed. We started off at the ER in Peru, IL and they decided to keep you overnight. You were not doing well, nor did we know how close to death you were. The nurse came in and couldn't even get a blood pressure on you. They worked on you for hours to get you coherent. I remember going into the room next-door after they couldn't find your blood pressure and declaring life into you. I knew I needed to call our Pastors, who ended up meeting us there and praying with me in the early hours of the morning. We were declaring and agreeing that the hospital in Peoria would find a bed in the critical care unit.

The doctor came in and told me that I needed to think about putting you on hospice. I would not hear of it. I told him that you were healed and that you were going to walk in there and let them see what our God did for you. I wouldn't let anyone speak anything over you that wasn't positive. I know they thought I was in denial, but I knew how powerful our God is! Within hours they found you a bed in the critical care unit, and you were on your way. Many of our family members and church family followed us from hospital to hospital and stayed to make sure we were covered on all levels. I don't think they will ever know how much that meant to us; just their mere presence brought comfort, strength, and healing.

I will never forget those times and I thank God for them. As the team of doctors came in and tried to get you stable, your lifeless body lay there, and tears were streaming down my face, I thought, "God touch him. He's fought for so long and he has trusted you with everything. Touch his body and make him whole!" There came a point that they took you off the TPN and did a surgery so that they could feed you through a tube past the tumors, so you could get strong enough to have chemo. I remember the look on your doctor's face when he came out and told us that the cancer had spread, and your whole inside was locking down. In that moment, I felt all the noise leave the room, and Papa holding my face in His hand, as my tears filled His palms. He said "I am with you. Do not be afraid. Breathe, my daughter."

I know many of us have gone through times where all the noise around us made us numb, and we just needed time to stop so we could breathe. If you are going through that time right now, I encourage you to take time in silence. Step back away from everything else and just listen to the Father. Sometimes words don't need to be spoken but the peace of our Father comes in and quiets all the chaos.

8

His Grace Was Sufficient

When you came back to your room and they told you what was going on, I'll never forget your words. You said, with a big smile on your face, "Well, it's out of man's hands now, and only in God's hands. I can't wait to see what He is going to do."

I remember the next morning the doctors wanted to have a meeting with us. They came in and told us that at most you only had six months to live, and that there was no other treatment that they could do to help you. I remember I felt so angry. How dare they come in like they were God and tell you when you were going to die! I was so upset I felt like I was in a bad dream, and at any minute I was going to wake up and everything was going to be back to normal.

The bad dream became a nightmare in the days ahead. I remember one of our dates we had at the hospital, watching some of our favorite movies. We were just laughing, talking, and carrying on like we didn't have a care in the world. It was almost like Papa gave us that time to connect like we hadn't been able to do for a very long time. We held hands and I lay upon your chest. These are moments I will never forget.

When we left critical care to come home, you were feeling pretty good. They got all your levels up. Your body was starting to heal. We had 4 days of "normal. "

I remember the last time we went to the cancer center your incision had opened and this awful smell was leaking out of it. We had spent the whole night before in the ER in Peru, and they decided to take you to CCOA. They were going to give you blood transfusions because your blood levels were really low, which led me to believe that you had a gastrointestinal bleed. After you were settled, I went to a hotel room to sleep. It had been days since I had closed my eyes. You didn't tell me until I got back to the hospital that the doctor said there was nothing more they could do.

I remember the next day all of the doctors wanted to see us. I couldn't bear to hear what they were going to say, but nonetheless they wanted me there, and they told us both that there was no hope, and you needed to be on hospice. We called our kids in to let them know that they weren't going to pursue any other treatment. My heart hit a wall of pain. Never in my life could I even imagine this situation. I wondered what you were feeling during those days in the hospital, thinking and resting. At this point it was all in Papa's hands, and you knew that. You wanted me to rest, to trust, to believe. I thought about so many things, Babe. I held so tight to His hands as I felt life leaving you, the life of your body as you began to let go of it here and embrace it there. The light that once burned so bright began to dim that weekend. There was no worry or fear in you, just peace as I watched you sleep. I remember the song that kept playing in my head, "It's Your breath in my lungs, so I pour out my praise, I pour out my praise on You."

I believe that worship is one of the strongest weapons of defense against the enemy in any situation that anyone could face. *What are some of the songs that carried you through some of the darkest places that you've encountered?*

____

____

____

____

____

____

____

____

____

Even as the darkness was so evident, it brought life, growth, and perseverance to begin a change. It felt as if nothing was going on. You were cradled in a position that left you most vulnerable to trust the creator to guide you through the darkest of nights. We would begin to push and stretch out as the space started to become too small. We were so uncomfortable and felt as if we were running out of room. We almost felt trapped in our old selves but in that moment, I felt a sudden change. Though the darkness was prominent, the cocoon began to break open and light began to shine through. I noticed a difference in my being. It began to push out and rip out these beautiful, colorful, most splendid set of wings that were now a part of me. I began to flutter. It was most strengthening as the Son began to beam down, filling my heart full of hope. He whispered," Sometimes the darkness you find yourself in is where the most growth happens, when you are hidden away from all that has affected you and it is just Me and you, when you allow Me to change and transform what I always knew you could be. Embrace the change; embrace the wings and fly higher than you ever imagined you could."

"But what if I fall?" Oh, my dear, but what if you fly? Trust is a big deal. *What is one thing in which Papa is asking you to trust Him? Faith and trust go hand in hand. Write some things down in which you are wanting to trust God.*

____

____

____

9
When Trusting Him Sounded Like a Foreign Idea

I have been in this place before. It has become most familiar to me. I have taken many different paths, but they have led me here in different ways.

It seems to be hidden, a path that leads me here but this time, something is different. This time something is clearer. I look around knowing you are here, not so much looking inward and trying to understand, but opening my heart and putting out my hand. You come with that smile beaming all around. As the light grows brighter, I see all that was lost has been found. You whispered as You twirled around me, "The darkness you saw, the darkness you have been in, was coming from the disappointment that lies within. The path kept leading you here because, My Child, you had to see it clearly. You tried to push it all down and pretend you were okay, but I knew the truth that kept you away. I know you think you trust Me, but some things along the way have tainted your view of Me as I lead you through. Your perspective has changed. You don't see Me with the same wide-eyed wonder, just waiting for Me to take your hand. The disappointments along the way have caused you to look inward so you could figure out the way. Oh, I know you love Me, long for Me, but I also see the hidden anger from inside. My Child, you don't see the big picture, just little pieces of the journey. Trust Me to bring you through. Trust Me to know the plans I have for you."

As I took His hand, I knew that all His heart was for me. I knew I had to look past what my natural eye saw into what was there form the beginning of time: the One who holds My future, the One who holds time.

He was right. I think as Christians we don't want to admit that we have anger inside us. We want to push it all down and pretend it isn't there. How can I be mad at God? It is quite simple. I believed God was going to move the way I thought He should, and when He didn't, I was confused, frustrated, and scared. The problem was, I had painted a picture of how it was all going to be turned around and really didn't come to Him and surrender to His bigger picture, nor did I know how my husband felt about what was going on. I just knew I wanted Papa to fix it and get back to life as normal. Life wasn't ever going back to normal the way I imagined it should. This journey was going to be one of great surrender and trust. It would cause my eyes to be opened to the greater purpose and plan He had.

This journey has proven to be one that has stripped me of who I thought I was. My strengths soon became my deep weakness. What I thought I knew has left an empty void in my soul, leading me on a path I never wanted to travel. I cried out to You deeper than I have ever cried before. It came from deep within the hidden parts of the caverns of my soul. The places I thought were open to Your heart led me to this broken place. It's funny in a way, how we think we have opened ourselves up to You, how deep down inside we only let You through the screen door. The big heavy door to those places in me I never would have thought were only skin deep. I tucked those places far from my sight, but the trials of this journey have made them come to the light. It's raw and real as I finally let You in, no longer holding them like a winner's trophy. I used to believe that I had the control, but little did I know as it took root it gained the very parts I wasn't willing to let go. It gained strength and began to build a wall between the truth of Your love and the lies of which it was made. I never fully understood that the very thing I thought I was protecting was the very thing that was trying to destroy me. I've learned on this journey my deep need for You and how Your love really healed those places I tried to hide from you. The painful road that opened my eyes to You, has taken me deeper to the roads that were designed by You. Learning to rest has become a great weapon of truth. I hold those times in my heart as the world's chaos tries to deafen Your voice, leaning into Your frequency, listening to Your still small voice. It has led me to those places where words are not enough. You have begun to pour out Your passion on me as my heart is now open to receive all You said I could be. I am no longer lost in this world's embrace, knowing I'm a child of Your amazing Grace.

What are the things you think you have hidden from God? Ask Holy Spirit to show you and help you to let it go. This may be a difficult thing, but it will open your heart and release the enemy's hold on you.

10

When Questions Arise and Answers are Scarce

In the book of Psalms, it shows us that there were times in David's life that he questioned God and let out all his frustrations, but always came back by saying, "but I know You are greater than all my feelings." David's heart was real, raw, and true to His God. Here is a scripture I have often come across in this journey and held it close.

"Here's what I've learned through it all: Don't give up; don't be impatient; be entwined as one with the Lord. Be brave and courageous, and never lose hope. Yes, keep on waiting—for he will never disappoint you!" Psalms 27:14 The Passion Translation

What we think is a disappointment is really an opportunity to see beyond the natural eye into what He sees. It's about trusting when we don't understand. God is good even when our situations are not.

I wrote this text to my husband that day the doctors wanted me to let him go home on hospice. I thought if I let that happen, I was giving up on him. It is a painful reminder of how frail we are in the flesh and how much we need Papa's strength.

Sun, Apr 9, 4:57 PM

I don't want to lose you honey ... I'm just so tore up right now I feel like I have to faith and I know that doesn't please God

:(honey I love you and it's gonna be ok. You need to cry babe

Honey your my rock, my best friend God promised He would not disappoint me but these people want you to go home and die babe

Who cares what they Say God says something different

I love you with all my heart ❤️

Mon, Apr 10, 8:19 PM

I love you babe ❤️ please play those scriptures over you as you sleep

I knew I couldn't cry because I wouldn't stop, but my husband knew I needed to break. He knew I needed to let go of everything that was holding me in this place. A place where the enemy thought he was going to overtake me. I felt so lost in that moment. I cried out to God and asked Him to strengthen me because I felt like I was going to lose it.

Then His peace came and flooded both our souls. You drifted off to sleep as I held your hand. I looked at your face and couldn't help but see the strength you had. I sat there with tears streaming down my face as I wrote this note to you.

"I noticed yesterday the struggle you felt when you looked at the circumstances and they overwhelmed you. I saw your heart as it began to weep, crying out to Papa to get some relief. I saw how you pressed through even though you didn't feel like it. I saw the pain and fatigue try to take you down, but you wouldn't have it. You wanted to break through. I saw the weakness your body felt, but you wouldn't stop; you just kept crying out. I saw the sleepless nights of just wanting rest. I saw how you worshiped your way through trusting that He knew best. I saw how you wept for a moment and wanted to give up and you were just done, but you wouldn't stay there. You began to speak out.

I saw you today, getting stronger. You wouldn't back down in defeat but kept on walking, standing on His feet. He walked you through the toughest of days and now He is putting a song inside your soul. You rested in His arms, and He spoke deeply to your soul! I saw a hero being made. I saw a warrior taking his place. I saw my husband pressing through, and I want you to know I'm so very proud of you. You are an inspiration to me"

11
The Quiet Before the Storm

We came home a few days later and not much was said. That month was the most we had been home in months. I was able to do all that you needed medically so you wouldn't have to go back and forth, and there were no more treatments to have.

During the month of April, I felt as if God gave us the time to just breathe. We spent time together and were strengthened in our faith. Our church family came over and lightened our load. They brought a breath of fresh air and strength. I truly don't know where we would be without our church family, our family, and friends. Our grandkids would come over and bring such a smile to your face.

Livy Sue had to be right where you were. She never wanted to leave your side when she was over. She brought her iPad and talked to you for hours. I know she wanted to help you in any way she could.

Easter came and we had a nice dinner with family. I emptied your bag as they visited, and I noticed that there were clumps of blood clots. So, I called the doctor and he sent over the nurse. You were throwing up nonstop, even though you hadn't eaten or drunk anything. They wanted to send you to the hospital to get you on medication, so they put you in the ICU to regulate everything.

I remember the doctor coming in to talk to your mom, Jerry, and me. He said, "Mrs. Evans, you can keep your husband alive through the TPN (which was his lifeline) for years, but he doesn't have good quality of life. You need to let him go." I looked at him and said, "I can't let him go. I know what God said and my husband is healed." He said he would keep you there until you didn't get sick anymore, which was for a few days. Because we didn't want you on hospice, all the other doctors wouldn't send you home with pain meds because it had to go through your port. This doctor knew you were going to need pain meds and knew I could put you on hospice. I believe in my heart that this doctor gave me time to understand what was going on. He sent you home with pain meds and he sent a nurse over to teach me how to administer it. I had to give you meds every hour of the day. Kayla helped me when I grew tired. You started running a fever the evening of Mother's Day. The nurse was going to come check on you that Monday.

That Mother's Day was the last holiday we spent together. You came out on the porch in a reclining chair that Ben took outside for you, and we planted flowers and you told us where you wanted those to go. We didn't know it then, but the following Tuesday we had to make the decision to send you to a hospice home to regulate your medication.

We sat outside until the stars came out, enjoying the sounds of summer. I think back on that time, and I just can't believe how gracious God was to us. The kids all had their time with you. We laughed, were silly, and for that moment forgot what was going on and felt like our old selves.

12

The Storm Came and So Did Papa!

Tuesday morning came and the nurse wanted to talk to us both. He wanted you to go into the hospice home for them to regulate your meds. You asked me what I thought, and I told you that this was a decision that you would have to make because they wanted to take you off the TPN. I knew I couldn't make that decision. You said, "Babe, God can heal me even if I'm not on the TPN," and you decided to go. The next two weeks I had to learn how to let go of you so you could embrace what was in front of you. I saw Papa in every moment of time. He never left us.

I remember driving to Peoria to the hospice home, our girls in the back seat, and both of us trying to explain what was going on. You took each of their phones and made a little video telling them how much you loved them and encouraging them. We were all crying, trying to hold back the tears as we arrived at the hospice home.

When we arrived, there was a nurse waiting with a wheelchair for us to use to bring you in. As soon as I pushed you into the home, I will never forget hearing you say, "Babe, I feel such peace here." It took me aback a little, because at that moment, even though I tried not to listen, I knew right then you were not coming home with me.

I had to sign papers that you were a DNR (do not resuscitate). It was so surreal. I felt so numb at that point. That night we all slept in your room, but honestly, there wasn't any sleeping. You were up vomiting, and in between we told stories and laughed.

The next morning, they were able to help you stop vomiting, and I asked you if it would be okay with you if the girls and I stayed at a hotel, just to breathe a little. Your mom came and stayed the night with you, and all the girls, Ben, Will, and the grandkids and I stayed in a hotel and talked about what was before us. We ate together and tried to sleep as much as we could.

I met with the doctor, and she told me in her opinion you wouldn't last but a week. You already showed signs of mottling. She said your heart was strong, so it would take a little bit. I remember when you asked me to give you your bath because you didn't want the nurses to do that for you. I was so grateful I had the opportunity to do that because within the next two days you fell asleep and didn't communicate much more.

But Papa gave us some blessings to hold us until we see you again. He kissed us with some precious moments. As I sat in silence one night in your room, I saw the long breaths you took and how so much was changing. Papa began to speak:

"Here, My Child, is the place where it's Me and you alone. Here is where I teach you how to truly rest in Me. We have come to this place where you will learn how to walk through the situations before you by using My word and trusting My heart. No one else will be able to walk this path with you, for I want to be the One the Only One to Whom you run. Here is where you will see who I really am. You will search the depths of Me for answers and you will learn to wait on My voice to lead you through the path that is laid before you. I invited you here because I know nothing else will satisfy your longing. You have cried out, "More, Lord!" and here I am wanting to give you more. I want your heart to rely completely on Me. I'm calling out to those places in you that have been hidden. They have been hidden away in disappointment, anger, stress, and unbelief. Oh, My Child, here is where your spirit will awaken to new life, vision, and purpose. Yes here, My Love, I will take those shattered pieces and put together the real you, the one you have hidden away behind the wall that you thought was protecting you. That wall, it didn't protect you but only kept you from seeing the truth. Here in this place is where My love will change your perspective so you can see what is right, real and reality. I invite you in to let go of all you are holding on to in this place in my heart that I have opened to you for revelation. Here we are, My Love. Will you come in?"

At that very moment I knew I wasn't going to be walking alone through anything that I had to face. He continued:

"I know what lurks in the deepest parts of your soul. It is something that has taken the life out of your living, the joy out of your laughter. It's the heaviness of yesterday's heartaches, the disappointment that comes when you try to carry the burden of blame that was never your fault. You held so tight to the picture of failure and what you thought was to be that the crack in the door allowed Satan in to speak. You, My Beautiful One, held tightly to his accusations because you took the burden upon yourself instead of just releasing it to Me. The ache in your heart has led to many walls being built, many walls that have left scars upon your heart. My Beautiful One, let go of Yesterday's lies and embrace the gift of today in all its truth. For even though I'm in your yesterdays, My power is in your today to equip you to see all that is before you. What you thought was dealt with has left a hole in your soul that can only be healed when you allow Me to put my finger on it and bring health back to the places that death has invaded. Allow Me to rend your heart, to tear it into pieces and then put it back together the way I always intended it to be. Trust the process, My dear one. Let go!"

What is hidden in your soul? What can you leave at the foot of the cross? *Let's take a moment and ask Holy Spirit to reveal what's in there and use the lines below to write it down.*

____

____

____

____

____

____

13
Great Victory Met a Great Battle

There are times that we truly begin to see what the Lord is saying when He said, "My thoughts are not your thoughts, nor are your ways My ways. For as the heavens are higher than the earth, so are My ways higher than your ways." In this journey I believe we all must come to a point where we are not trying to figure out the plan, we are not trying to control the plan and we are living in the moment, resting in His plan. Resting! Trusting! Knowing! He has it. We move forward with every step being revealed as we move. Nothing more, nothing less. When we try to figure it all

out and put our spin on what we think we know, we obstruct the will of God in our lives. Trusting is not doing what we think we know to do but to be led moment by moment in what He knows to be done.
When we try to figure out "Why this?" "Why that?" and "Why not?" it hinders our minds from hearing His still small voice. He is saying, "I have all your days in the palm of my hand. I know the plans I have for you. Rest in my love!"

I truly don't know what's in my future, but I know Who holds it. Even when we feel we have messed it up, He leads us to get back on the path He intended us to be on. "Trust! Rest! Know I am the Great I Am."

Keith passed away on the 25th of May at 3:32a.m., surrounded by his family singing worship songs as he took his last breath. His battle had ended, and he was in the arms of the One he loved.

As for me on the other hand, my battle had just begun. To say I was angry is an understatement. I never knew anger like that before. It was so deep and so intense. I just wanted to know why.

Have you ever been here? Let Holy Spirit speak deep inside your soul, allowing Him to bring anything that may be hidden to your attention. He knows you best and will lead you, not push you. Open up and allow Him to bring the healing waters your soul really needs.

____

____

____

____

14
Silence in War?

I think from my own experience, during the first year of grief you're numb, you have waves of overwhelming sadness, then you're numb again. In the second year you're trying to figure out where to go from here, who you are and what to do now. For me it was a loss of not only my husband, but one of my best friends. I was so angry that he was gone, so angry that Papa disappointed me and afraid of the raw feelings I was having.

How could I be angry at Papa? There was such a war going on inside of me. I know He is all powerful and He can do anything. So why didn't he heal Keith on this side of heaven? Why didn't he not keep His word? I was so confused, and I just couldn't grasp the truth. I stood on His word. I believed. I would not allow anyone or anything to speak any negativity over my husband. That's where the real battle began.

During the first year I battled with thoughts that I didn't pray enough, I didn't fast enough, I didn't believe enough. I didn't run to God like I had in the past. I was so distraught all my hope vanished. The very person I trusted most didn't do what I thought He was going to do.

Father this pain seems to be going deeper. The more I cry out, the more it seems to take me under. I've tried to let it all go, to push on without any hope. I just don't understand. Why would you take him when he was holding my hand? He was a gift you had given to me but took back, and now I can't breathe. I know in my mind You know better than I do, but this pain isn't going away no matter how hard I chase after You. These questions haunt me every single night, "Was he ready to leave here? Did he put up a fight? Did he know You were taking him away from us? Was his heart sad or was he just giving up? Did he feel your presence? Did you come for him? Was he scared or was he overjoyed? Did I do enough, or did I let him down? Did I believe enough, or did I somehow give up?" Father you know the deepest parts of me. Help me to trust you again as I did in the past. I love You, Father, even though I don't understand, even though I question everything that is at hand. I need You, Father, oh how I need You. Help me to see Your plan. Help me to rest and take hold of Your hand.

I came into your garden to breathe upon your soul, to speak life to those things that are dying. In the constant scorching of the sun and lack of rain to refresh its roots, I see the hinderances in your heart that seem to sprout up even though you pulled them out. You have buried disappointments and sorrow deep within your roots. Yesterday's disappointments have built a wall around your soul and your outlook through these pains is tainted. You see through the mud that has darkened your view; you let go of the light that was guiding you. I came to give life and breath upon your soul. I have always promised you I will never let you go. You must choose what your next step will be. Will you trust in Me so you will be at rest? The circumstances that have left you numb have brought a death to your soul that's hindering your growth. Your love for Me is bringing life to the topsoil, but I desire to go deep into your roots so strength will come when the winds of life blow harder. I wait for your voice to cry out My name. I will come running and I will bring the latter rain. Choose life and begin to really live, for great things will come in the midst of all of it. For now, I see new petals beginning to grow life that will replace the lifeless hope. You have blocked the nourishment of My word to your heart. You have grown weak and sickly in Your soul. You walk around lifeless, with artificial hope. Everything you chose to give you life has left you raw and malnourished. Have I not said that I have come to give life and to give it more abundantly? Choose life and begin to live. Hope again, dream again, and believe again.

Do you know that His love for you will keep on flowing even though you are angry, disappointed, and frustrated? He knows you even better than you know yourself. Even though your journey may be in the valley or off the beaten path, one cry from your heart and He is there with arms opened wide.

15
When He Holds You Close

I remember one night my 18-year-old daughter texted me this and it really ministered to my heart, because before the time of his illness, she had been far from the Lord, and through all of this she saw her dad finish well.

"No one at the funeral ever said how good God was. I find that weird. God knew what was going to happen to dad before he was even a thought in Grandma and

Grandpa's head. Dad lived out God's plan and then some. The night we found out he had cancer, I feel like that was God telling dad, "This is your last trial." And dad encouraged everyone's faith and remained faithful. Until God said it was more than good enough, and it was time to come home. I just find it weird that no one said that God was good. Because even though He did take dad, it was God's time to take him. God's plan with dad had ended and God wanted him back. God is good. Idk. I feel like it was weird."

One thing I spoke out loud after my husband died was that I was going to church to worship like I never had before. I knew in my mind that if I didn't do that there would be a wall between me and Papa. I wanted to show the enemy I wasn't walking away from Father God no matter the grief I felt inside.

In every problem we face there is a promise. As I began to meditate on the word and ask the Lord to show me what He was saying in His word about those whose lives I had been studying (David, Joseph), He began to reveal His hidden truths. How many of us have heard this scripture from Jeremiah 29:13, "You will seek Me and find Me when you search for Me with all your heart." Jeremiah 29:13 *Scripture quotations taken from the (NASB®) New American Standard Bible®, Copyright © 1960, 1971, 1977, 1995, 2020 by The Lockman Foundation. Used by permission. All rights reserved.*

In every situation we face, in every crisis, in every hurt, disappointment or circumstance the Lord is inviting us to search for Him in all of this so He can reveal Himself in a whole new way to us. You see, the Lord has many facets. He is not just 3 dimensional as we often see things; He has many dimensions to who He really is. In every problem there is a promise that

He spoke before the foundations of the world. He already made a way before you were facing the problem. It says in His word that He really knew you and He formed you. He knew what you would face, and He made a promise for you to grab ahold of and speak out. His word is His promise. It is packed with power and authority. It is also packed with truth and identity. You see, if you knew what the enemy knows about who you are then you would know that you win. You have a promise and can overcome! We get so lost and distracted by what we see in the natural that we never dig deeper into the promises He spoke. We try to fight through on our own. We rest in our own capabilities and try to figure it all out. We miss who The Lord is to us in that situation. Jesus always depended on the word from His Father then He moved out into it. Every situation He faced He sought His Father's face and there is where He received the promise to move powerfully and in the authority of heaven.

Let's pause here and pray. What is He speaking to your heart?

____

____

____

____

____

____

____

I have been on this journey for four years and I have truly seen the faithfulness of Papa. I've had to totally start from the beginning. I have amazing people all around me. My spiritual parents have walked me through some of the darkest days and kept reminding me that Papa had a plan. My prayer for all of you who have read this is that you will open yourself up to Papa and trust that whatever you are experiencing He will lead you and strengthen you through it all.

You walked into the room where I lay upon the floor. I felt Your presence as You came through the door. You held me in Your arms as the tears began to flow and collected every one of them as they came forth. I heard Your heart as I lay upon Your chest. You spoke to mine even though no words were said. You felt every sorrow as it came up, all the questions that were buried, all the strength that felt lost. You never hurried the process, You never gave up but held me even tighter as my soul released it all. In times of grief where words don't make sense, where nothing that is spoken can bring true rest, Your silence is soothing to the chaos in my soul. Your love for me never lets go. It's in this weakness where everything is raw, where fear tries to come in and cause me to fall. It's here where You take my face in your hands and speak a whisper to my soul, "Peace, be still," to the storm that feels out of control. In that moment it becomes still. All my thoughts become clear, and hope returns where there was once fear. You heard my silent cries from deep within. You came running when I spoke Your name. You broke every wall I tried to build, thinking I was protecting myself. You knew me very well. You spoke the truth deep in my soul, telling me I would make it through.

I couldn't see past the pain but rode the waves of grief. Your love held me up as my soul began to breathe. I stopped fighting against the waves of grief and just surrendered to lying in Your arms as you took the lead. As I looked up to those eyes of peace, I saw the tears begin to flow on Your cheeks as the words you spoke set my heart free.

www.ingramcontent.com/pod-product-compliance
Ingram Content Group UK Ltd.
Pitfield, Milton Keynes, MK11 3LW, UK
UKHW021931200726
13853UKWH00010B/52

9 798797 528333